OCEANS ALIVE

Sea Urchins

by Martha E. H. Rustad

BELLWETHER MEDIA • MINNEAPOLIS, MN

Note to Librarians, Teachers, and Parents:

Blastoff! Readers are carefully developed by literacy experts and combine standards-based content with developmentally-appropriate text.

Level 1 provides the most support through repetition of high-frequency words, light text, predictable sentence patterns, and strong visual support.

Level 2 offers early readers a bit more challenge through varied simple sentences, increased text load, and less repetition of high frequency words.

Level 3 advances early-fluent readers toward fluency through increased text and concept load, less reliance on visuals, longer sentences, and more literary language.

Level 4 builds reading stamina by providing more text per page, increased use of punctuation, greater variation in sentence patterns, and increasingly challenging vocabulary.

Level 5 encourages children to move from "learning to read" to "reading to learn" by providing even more text, varied writing styles, and less familiar topics.

Whichever book is right for your reader, Blastoff! Readers are the perfect books to build confidence and encourage a love of reading that will last a lifetime!

This edition first published in 2008 by Bellwether Media.

No part of this publication may be reproduced in whole or in part without written permission of the publisher. For information regarding permission, write to Bellwether Media Inc., Attention: Permissions Department, Post Office Box 1C, Minnetonka, MN 55345-9998.

Library of Congress Cataloging-in-Publication Data
Rustad, Martha E. H. (Martha Elizabeth Hillman), 1975–
  Sea urchins / by Martha E.H. Rustad.
    p. cm. – (Blastoff! readers. oceans alive)
Summary: "Simple text and supportive images introduce beginning readers to Sea Urchins. Intended for students in kindergarten through third grade"—Provided by publisher.
  Includes bibliographical references and index.
  ISBN-13: 978-1-60014-109-6 (hardcover : alk. paper)
  ISBN-10: 1-60014-109-9 (hardcover : alk. paper)
  1. Sea urchins—Juvenile literature. I. Title.

  QL384.E2R87 2008
  593.9'5–dc22   2007009798

Contents

Sea urchins are ocean animals.
They come in many colors.

Sea urchins live on the ocean floor. They can also live on rocks or **coral reefs**.

Sea urchins are covered
with sharp **spines**.

They have a hard shell under their spines. A sea urchin's shell is left behind after it dies.

tube feet

Sea urchins have hundreds of **tube feet**. Each one has a tiny **sucker** on the tip.

Sea urchins use tube feet
to breathe in water.

Sea urchins use their tube
feet and spines to move.

Their suckers also help them move. They pull the sea urchin along the ocean floor.

Sea urchins move slowly
in search of food.

Sea urchins eat **seaweed**, small animals, and a kind of ocean life called **algae**.

mouth

A sea urchin's mouth is on the bottom of its body.

Five teeth scrape food
into its mouth.

Some fish and animals such as sea otters like to eat sea urchins.

Sea urchins can hide in
rocks or sand. They use
their spines to dig.

Some sea urchins have **poison** in their spines.

They can **sting** fish or animals to try to scare them away.

Sea urchins can grow as wide
as 12 inches (30 centimeters).

Sea urchins can live a long time. Some are more than 100 years old!

Glossary

algae—tiny living things that grow in the water

coral reef—a structure in the ocean made of the skeletons of small ocean animals called corals

poison—a substance that can hurt or kill another living thing; the poison in sea urchins hurts but does not usually kill other living things.

seaweed—a plant that grows in ocean waters

spine—a hard and sharp part on a plant or animal

sting—to hurt with a sharp body part; sea urchins sting with their poison spines.

sucker—a rounded body part that helps an animal stick to something

tube feet—thin, flexible body parts sea urchins use to move and breathe

To Learn More

AT THE LIBRARY
Gilpin, Daniel. *Starfish, Urchins, and Other Echinoderms*. Minneapolis, Minn.: Compass Point Books, 2006.

Hirschmann, Kris. *Sea Urchins*. Detroit, Mich.: KidHaven Press, 2005.

Rake, Jody Sullivan. *Sea Urchins*. Mankato, Minn.: Capstone Press, 2007.

Schaefer, Lola M. *Sea Urchins*. Chicago, Ill.: Heinemann Library, 2004.

ON THE WEB
Learning more about sea urchins is as easy as 1, 2, 3.

1. Go to www.factsurfer.com

2. Enter "sea urchins" into search box.

3. Click the "Surf" button and you will see a list of related web sites.

With factsurfer.com, finding more information is just a click away.

Index

The photographs in this book are reproduced through the courtesy of: NOAA, front cover; Juniors Bildarchiv/Alamy, p. 4; David Fleetham/Alamy, p. 5; Images & Stories/Alamy, p. 6; Alex James Bramwell, p. 7; Marevision/Age fotostock, pp. 8-9, 11; Juan Carlos Calvin/Age fotostock, p. 10; Georgie Holland/Age fotostock, pp. 12, 13; Visual & Written/Alamy, pp. 14, 21; Michal Adamczyk/Dreamstime, p. 15; Tom Mangelsen, p. 16; Andre Seale/ imagequestmarine.com, p. 17; Andre Seale/Age fotostock, p. 18; Sanamyan/Alamy, p. 19; tbkmedia.de/Alamy, p. 20